SUSAN BLANSHARD

POEMS

QUIETER HISTORIES
Winter to Winter

PAGE ADDIE PRESS
UNITED KINGDOM

CONTENTS

ANTARCTICA

A block of ice floats faster than a stone
The killer whale follows the seal
When wind is in the east
Then fishes bite the least

First you are carpenter of ice
Hearing the whole world splice
Wind is in the south
Blows bait in the fish's mouth

Wintertime with blood and brine
Rich fruit cake and potted ham
Bottled peach and pilchard can
Mules will carry your provisions

Marrowbones and lardy tins
Sou'wester from a whale foreskin
Boil tallow and fat will follow
Blow the wind loud and fast

It will lower at the final blast
The longest day and shortest night

Snuff out candle, shut the light
Preserves and wine outlive our marrow

Come when it will, it comes tomorrow
The raven with a sack of sorrow
The mast, gaff and the boom
Glaciers lay like grander ruins

All things eventually lose solid value
One's unlucky, two's lucky
Three's health, four's wealth
Five is weather thick and thin

Six seized flag with its useful stars
Thick cloth endures anything
When wind is in the west
Then fishes bite the best

Lose a minnow to catch a whale
Catch them on Sunday your safety seek
Storm shall have you rest of the week
Slip on the same ice, twice in old boots

During the curfew of pack-ice hum
Mules die, sled dogs succumb one by one
Wasted last saliva on a postage stamp

Last letter back to the mainland

Thank you for your blackberry jam
Was never bitter and never sweet
Wife take care of our newborn
Look for nightshade in new wine

Children look after your mother
Walk fast in snow, in ice walk slow
In extremes of heat and cold
When ice and snow are both together

Sit by burning logs and save boot-leather
Books and friends should be few
Bread of pleasure, drink of measure
All sorts of perishables and survival rations
Rob royal bees and leave us honey-less
Empty hive and sweet impoverishing
Our bread dipped in dirty water.

Beyond the ship of sailor boys
The night-man speaks to the night
Come out all you black storms
The snow shall speak for the ice

Dark rum toddy says the sailor boy
Is drunk from a beaten cup
Your deeds earned crown nor wreath
Now the punishment book is shut.

THE HELM

First you are a sailor on the ship
of the miraculous—

Gold in the morning, silver at noon
Mast, gaff and boom, this altered room
Under the burden of canvas and wood—
God saves the dog from ruby moon
Then you left the rudder with its tiller
Bent, breathless under gold heirlooms
And seizing a rich man's look
Empty as the devil's prayer book
Then you are a carpenter saved by screw and nail
God saves the wild dog chasing its tail
Aphrodisiac on one hand, narcotic on the other—
if you lose a shadow, beware of its opposite.

MANNERS OF FISH

Above the bay shaped like a back-bone
Rows of houses for sugar factory workers
The closeness of rooms and unmade beds
Now the unharvested beets gone to seed
Why did you only want perfect
Of child about you
That he never forgot anything
That he never broke anything
For what I know
He was always at dinner table
Half an hour before mealtimes
All the time to wait incognito
There his fingers made shadow figures
On the far wall—a rabbit, a mouse
And a face that opened and closed its mouth
Like a drawing of the sun
The serious faces of children
It was only a small part of life
One of many circles
What good is a smile if a mouth won't hold it.
Wouldn't it have been easier to love?

REVERIE FOR MEMORIES

And here the house so near the sea
And here bare form beneath the sand
To feel the always coming on
The always rising of his hand

To feel gnawed out the hopeless bay
The knitted coils of rope and cold
To take wave by wave the absent struggle
As an empty sea destroys the coral

Or maybe all the waves lost momentum
And there is a nothing less than stillness
And the wound lays naked to the moon
On a spurious glitter of shifting sand

Out there in the dark, there's a wild tattoo
Of a thousand rocks rebelling
But soon the tide returning
The voice of salt drowns out the thought

And now there is talk inside the home
One thing braver than another
And how a house is not a boat

And how a boat is not a ship

It's not my fault if I am a child

When he comes here again
That I may see him changed
Like a dream from which together
We awake and rub our eyes

But his wool coat remains folded
Now the grave markers rise like islands
No forgiveness for his acts to destroy us
Crepitation owns the growing grass

And there seems to be a silence
But it is silence with a deeper sound—
it is a wind that means nothing.

Smokey Cape Lighthouse

Anyone died in a bright lighthouse
with up so stepping many bricks high
rain, wind, storms, the overly lonely
they talk local swore she'd haunt she would
glow-worm tapers seaweed vapors on the shore

Anyone died in the pretty villa
with weatherboards wide so painterly white
have lived for breath, to die not at all
little by little nursery is a widow's room
what lacerates fog stirs the mist

Any birds left in dovecote
white sailing when they did their waltz
busy birds wish for straw in spring
side by side, deep and deep
names slip by and by

The more they dream the more they sleep
stop start all the sick, old or dead forgot the reason
others look away until only the stars remember
and empty rooms are filled again.

OMEN

The fantail flew inside the house
Entered by closed door
I did not know what to perceive
Bird of warning lest something go wrong

Or the bird of nature,
The cloak of feathers
Or just after
Darkness deeps the long hallway

The shadow of bird crossing to and fro
Weaving the tribal coat of consequences
Feathers trace inexplicable course
Symbols and tools stenciled on the wall

Or the bird of nature
The cloak of feathers
Or just after
Darkness deeps the long hallway

Like sun rays reached after the rain stops
Or a tongue that does not rust

Words and feathers the wind carries away
It was the face of a man left behind—
his hair the color of ashes.

THE STREAM

In my Brother's house there are many mansions—
The Master in a studio on second floor
Four walls papered blue, always blue
It seemed to be from a private life
That makes one distinct impression
Far distant, a painting of Monet's water-lilies
No matter a fishing stream at Giverny
That even when he swam in some cold water,
Always the dreamer, believer of simple water,
A measure of scale, there were gold fish
Out of air, swallowing all memory
So the baited hook begins again—
is it possible for fish to love the fisherman?

TWO BROTHERS IN THE FIELD

Mostly there is no conversation
between the whistle of wild foxes
A shot from hunter's gun
Or snap of a rabbit snare
Breaking somber bones
It is the way of the countryside
You can walk the woods alone
Between lavender and sunflower fields
Where the two brothers are watching
Comings and goings
And that's how we were
Coming and going
Once key is handed over
Surname fades on gate
Some said the harder you fall
The easier to climb back up
Others thought happiness deserves loss
As if to clear the tears of the world
Like sun rays after rain stops
As gavel falls the screw turns
But impossible to retract the steps
Past mauve and yellow fields
I no longer ask directions
When two brothers turn away.

HATHAWAY COTTAGE

Acorn and hawthorns carved into the mantle
Doorway of poet courting ghosts and blood
Lover of parchment and feather bed
Nocturnal blanket was mossy warm

He was a man with a cupboard full of folios
Quill-full of ink, and the scribbling of his hand
To him, it was as much as the river flowing
She was a woman who noticed these things.

As bees are to candle wax, fire is to flame
His breath passed from her lips as all things
Mercurial as stars swept from skies
By the reapers slight vagueness of hand

Five hundred years that passed along river
Forbidden seeds of Saxon wheat
The scythes half-moon of steel
Shaped the cutters hand to a fist

Knuckle the sedge into chevron
Wattle gives up its branches for walls

Whatever is secured by hazel sticks
Burns slowly like a closed book

Late summer as blades of lawnmower
Cut through grass and lark song
Until dew has but one leaf to cling to
Enough to make diamonds in grass

To make you a necklace of hoarfrost—
at the wrong time of year.

STRATFORD-UPON-AVON

There was no need to hurry
Fortuna and the mystery
In this alchemy between lovers
All lovers young, all lovers must

Those who remember skin and musk
The girl who brought you luck
In sepia lights warm shadows
To enter the spell imagine—

So if the skin remembers
Raw silk quilt on the bed
Trailing tendrils and tiny leaves
Embroidered birds of paradise hover

Blindfolded figures guard the bearer
Mimosa outlined by pearls
As seeds on the hearts pattern
If our body has lost original outline

And everything we touch unravels—
If our love, like life, is non-returnable

Take this libidinous quilt from this bed
Cut one pattern for our shroud

Gather the two of us together
With tight binding stitches.

WAYS OF SEEING SNOW

Cold burred against the upstairs windows
Snowflakes etched ruby glass
Over the spine of ridge sun's red daggers
Broke through the winter's hag-like plums

Crocus in the alchemy of hoar frost
Mauve white the morphing bulbs
A woman cutting blue climbing rose
Caught the conditions of light

Later I see her walk to the village
I see her standing silent for the longest time
A condition of thought this sadness in her face.

When silence is a confession—
the snow stays silent.

FOR A PLURALIST

We were richer but not better off
Since we ransacked untouched tombs
Flint axes, bronze swords, roman coins
Small glass tiles of a wild dog on hind legs
And its lips drawn back

All frozen bones rattle
And beyond that—
Barren bone in chronological decline
Etched on scrimshaw by time

One or two clay pipes unearthed
Some figures like winged children
Little tiny idols—
Circles though small are quite complete
Clay-earth whitened by seasons

There was a dull sound of peach wood
Bearing children in the singing blossoms
New moon held the old in her arms
Before blandishments of sleep

Now she will and then she will not
The dead travel fast and if our ashes could wait
A thin column of mist rose up from her breath
As snow fell on higher ground

Twin scapula's felt below the collarbone
As a future transmutation
A few angelic tones
Foretold from the mouth of Angels'—
twisting her hair in whiteness.

WINTER SOLACE

As snow falls on high places—

The birds have gone
Between the fruitless autumn
One frozen garden to another
There were crisp twitters, snaps, and whistles

Between the fruitless autumn
They survived. No need for quiet
There were crisp twitters, snaps, and whistles
I don't remember all the chorus

They survived. No need for silence
There was the usual sedated landscape, cold
apothecary
I don't remember all the chorus
At the edge of wood, the carrion crow shivering

There was the usual sedated landscape, the cold
apothecary
Grateful there were no wolves
At edge of the wood

And if the all birds were shivering
They kept quiet about it

At no time did they think of missed migration
Or fear the end of all four seasons
And if the frozen ground was pitiless
They kept silent about it

They gathered in bare branches of hag-like trees
They were cold
What steel cage would ever know their stories

They gathered in branches in the hag-like trees
They were cold
What steel cage would ever know their story
As winter went on, reconfiguring the still-life season

Somewhere beyond winter lives the spring
The life of tree knew apple's white blossom
They did not know what cold was
Life of the tree knew apple's white blossom

They felt perhaps the young child's climbing
They had heard the cry of the young child's falling
They had felt the branches breaking—
as snow falls.

THE ALLOTMENT

The gardeners with barrows and spades
Arrived with the sun, for the planting
Rows of pear trees as honey bees dancing
Carry pollen before first blossoming

A memory of last year's harvest
Spare our littered thoughts
The sourness of unripe fruit
The taste of impatience

Would you give me if I took less
Pippin apples without pips
Would you give me if I took some?
So we tramped through the orchard
Until late summer, grass overgrown
More and more ripening needs
The stone-less plum was ours alone.

Summer Orchard

Whoever unlocked far gate
Sprayed measures of defoliate
True blight makes for rotten cores
We do not ask to be happy

Such completeness invites loss
To make a cursory visit
There was no catafalque
There lies this newborn

Sleeping in the statuary garden
Green cul-de-sac of funerary grass
Cherubim holding scarlet flowers
Andromeda bound in marble ribbon

Shifts her perpetual gaze to honey-bees
Who escaped their wicker hives
Settling on her polished hand
All men fear sextant and spade

One grave nearer the apiary
More than a child, afraid of bees

Disturbed by the dynamo of darkness
Shift rusted fingers of recent thought
All seeds grow in dark furlong
It was a full day.

WARWICKSHIRE

On medieval ground in shadow
Near the heart of the land
This is my true home
Now for a moment

Your face appears
From midnight till morning
Something to explain an exile
For the years were tragedies

Cut down like royal roses
One way or another
In one strike of a spade
The rose found its casket

It was long and complicated
Now blue china, wedding band
Fragments are found like a prayer
And you don't regret it?
Such was our practiced lips
In touch with the land, we wait our turn—
to plant a kiss through the stone.

THE WEIGHT OF ATTACHMENT

Re-illuminate the vault of heaven
And light us our destined course
By way of heavenly muse,
Who finds us before our birth
Move more heaven than earth
Carry away by years unfolded
The ruins of this almighty prison
The meaning of terrific thoughts
Chrysanthemums on iron crosses
As Empire cheats our ancestors
Encloses the future in shale and stone
You may think as that deep
Darkness intensifies
You are alone and unobserved
One is never alone
Virgo's like us are always born
In the cruelest part of winter
A song about bad weather and valor
Our five senses kept under a spell
This love for gold and gifts
An illusion of the most
Dangerous kind.

By Kitchen Door

A gardener knocks on the front door
Dark parameter of brewed coffee
And the way she holds bone china cup
As if watching roses turn to poems

An excuse to come into the hallway
Not to shelter from the morning
Or waste the day with frivolous endeavor
But to find his way into her room

And if man becomes her orchard
To sleep through winter and wake in spring
While all the while vines grow through
Certain walls of the room to cover truth

Like a whitewash of quicklime
Where truth is truly serpentine
And there is only an oak ladder
To the kitchen downstairs
Enough water is boiled
To make the coffee
That tastes of turpentine.

PILGRIM AVENUE

Left alone to count the saffron stamens
Or make figs into jam
But nothing brings enough money
Not honey from the hives, or windfall
Apples pressed to make cider
A woman leaves the house without knowing
What it is all about, she is so caught up in leaving
And therefore, closes the door on the shadows
Of things that belonged she can never forget
Sleeping in the bed which belongs to her body
Dreaming the dreams that belong to her mind
As figs turn ripe outside the kitchen door
There is not enough time left to make fig jam
Before drone of wasps intoxication
There is not enough time to make honey-wine—
but what secrets are left remain in my wrist pulse
And when I die...
Stay in the bones of my spine?
Leaves are falling from the vine
Pilgrims crosses are wrought of iron
So many prayers along the road.

Winter Garden in Lombardy

Through my life lover, I am left with traces of you,
Fragments felt in everything I touch—
Among the floral garden we are gardeners
The sun brooding its heat over the land
As it shortens our shadows
Before the months freeze over, a few winter roses
Planted by a hoarder, some say the color of custard
And what is this yellow envoy-it involves the soul
Some say the cowards yellow, to yell to cry out
To lay undisturbed, a handful of Emperor crocus
Dormant through perpetual winter, cold yellow
To dissolve and fade into the following year
Regenerate and live forever, perhaps beyond ordinary
In the house of finders' and keepers'
Here oak trees steal the daylight of winter's light
In such a disturbed atmosphere, the Holy fog
Moss covers the garden wall of the quiet city
Not so much verdant green in color of tapestry
More like the emeralds you kept in waxed paper
Until you whisper to the jeweler, turn emeralds into a
perpetual necklace—a week before our wedding.

In The Studio

You are by birth and from this hour,
I have hidden you and kept you
Whatever art and nature divine
Convert sun and moon to wine
As nights silence spreads out sable wings
To save our mansions from oblivion
The sound of sunlight a moment before
We will never close our eyes to this
If forever is an endless place
Your ears can hear and your eyes can see,
This human kind, open your arms
To hold the person that was meant to be.

ASTRONOMER'S NOTES

The rising moon of Venus
born a second time through the foam
exists like an illusion
in the argent of your mind

Those wishing to find silver
are always able to find
the moon rising from foreign seas
or the coming of another time

When Vesuvius lifts its snow
into the revolutionary skies
this beautiful illusion
does not change anything

It only seems to change the world
Nothing to do with a solitary thinker
For when you depend on omens
to divine all that is future
but all thoughts of yours are darkened
when the moon's behind a cloud.

ISLE OF WIGHT

Everyone says I remind them of someone—

Green as sage, my Grandfather's eyes
The reason the greenhouse is glass
The stones very human
Closer and hunters' guns shoot

By the river, and storms of such severity
Green iris in water-garden of visionary
One hand on glass, one on the bottle
A thousand grains of sand trickle through

But everything is a question of timing
Each hour is like a year of waiting
Like a dream tucked under a pillow
As unbidden shroud envelopes the earth

Whatever you know of endless lock down
Tell my own freewill the opposite.
Confined indoors delirious for sunlight
Compose a mental list of names and faces

Signatures of past, what we did cannot change
By the lines on my palm, a sense of past rooms
Doors left open as the Sage found each key
New wood door but rotting casement

Bricks and mortar, sunken basement
Dry rock walls of resurrection or renovation
So the sun forces the sleeper to move the hammock
Around the balcony, from place to place

While the wind keeps changing windows
Around the conservatory, pane by pane
Nothing breaks us more than nil explanation
The reason the greenhouse is glass

The stones very human
Green as sage, my Grandfather's eyes
Tall as my Father
Heart-broken as my Mother was
You held all my shadows
Our five senses kept under a spell
So says the Keeper of Life—

The first breath opens up the ribcage
The last breath twists the heart backwards.

THE WRECK-YARD

From every part of the known world
one highway unites one another
on the journey back to place of shadows
a house for sale, if it can find a buyer

you can walk a thousand miles
from the wreck-yard
mascara running down your face
far into dreams on a drowsy night

by hundreds of ways if you desire to do so
Friday night's dream, on Saturday night told
one's unlucky, two's lucky, four's wealth
much of life is about calculations

the whole is greater than the part
nothing without each other
a house continues to stand
after the builder has built

and water remains hot for some time
after the fire has ended

three's health, five's death,
a nail in the wound is sure to come true

as the hawk pursues the trembling dove
as I looked out for you
if you know one King, you know them all
if all things seen, are believed

bewitched our quieter histories
an age built up our house, an hour to destroy
in a moment the ashes were made
a house does not keep two dogs

to dig up buried retribution
but the house was a long time growing
there was a suggestion of error
a pretended tear can look sincere

now they tell of this prodigy,
the two who return from faraway lands,
there unheard-of icons of obscurity
and uncertain combinations of wealth—

all loss to and from, above and below
are calculated by the Master.

MISSIVE

Every house is a fable made of stone
covered with ivy on a single day
come what will, come what may
this blueprint of memory—

bees with hives on the sunny side
simple pergola in ivied space
woman shares this sidereal place
far from home is nearer to harm

how we fall into each other's arms
what stones do we need to re-build
a house & how many & what remembered
pattern, herringbone, like an ancient home

chaos of washing and wrung-out shirts
ink of sapphire, heart of rubies
holding prayer stones for centuries,
we will find stones of many colors and after,

never mind if these stones are real
stealing is cheaper than asking
gold watches on thin wrists—
we gained time instead of losing it.

WITH NIGHTSHADE

At first her love ever-changing
Like Heraclitus' luminous river
The velvet of expensive hotel
Trifles of silk and blue
Without regret or memory
A woman does not ask advice
Before she buys a wedding trousseau
Like Raphael's Madonna del Granduca
As every bride in amorous ritual
Until it faded blue like the masterpiece,
Between girl and woman, like Madonna's
Interesting scar, and it was sweet,
Bacillus of roses like buds
As Madonna del Granduca dress
Laid on the floor—
enter stranger and be happy.

THROUGH THE MASTERPIECE

Some diaries I burned in the fugitive years
Yet they were written in languages
Without a false note—
I burned them because they remembered too much.

But now half a century is serious
Nothing old enough to be antique
Examining the jewels through stolen loupe
Gold is gold, platinum is platinum

The saleable items left in the safe
Past days of luxury and give-a-ways
Hours which carry off years and days
Warned us against permanence

Dreams burning longer than desire
Milton's golden lyre plays to endless realms
There is nothing more dangerous
Than our dreams burning inside

In broken light of moon, inevitable winter
Laughter in the top room, find your touch in the dark

How this kind of captivity kept us together
Whenever I listen to the old songs,
Repeat the story from the beginning—
In the end it is impossible not to become
What others believe we are.

VELLUM

The first books were from quiet lands

The house in dark city half deaf half blind
To share a key with the lost ones
Image of trophy house in fragments
But one of the homeless unlocked the gates

One of them able to build a gable with snow
Forge window-panes of hoar frost
Imagination compares, it never creates
White arches of solitude, white bells of mistletoe

The quiet books were from other lands
We derive no satisfaction in figments

I place a table under almond tree
Old branches spread out like arms
Songbirds come at the wrong time of year
And deafen us with their tune

But birds cast the fever over far lands

And landmarks fall with the blossom
Clots the earth like rose-tinted granite

The mourning doves left in the city

By their song we could hear somber bells
But we baked bread in sun's heat
For all you give away is saved for you
We ate bread, in ceremony with wild birds—

I do not know how things have happened.

CHERUBIM

Your desk covered with quieter memories
There, the flock of birds you kept above
Flutter and sang around your head
Taking seeds from your outstretched hands
Like Assisi in the Garden of Goodness
I watch as you pick up falling feathers
Tie them into a feather brush
All you give away on earth is kept for you,
All you keep is lost
The curse remains in the seeds
And when you think no one is will see
You paint the undreamed bird
Eyes as green as nasturtium seeds
You paint the canary feathers—
Like a dead yellow chrysanthemum,
That might be thrown away.

VERDE

I met a man who spoke Spanish
talked about scraps of things in gypsy words
pieces of gold/doves/moon, a shirt
a thief, those who steal at dusk

guns, candles. This man
(smile) how good it was to make
some conversation... commandments
the fingers, saint asleep/to rob a person asleep,

lanterns/eyes a spy, and dancing/to take flight
I had been looking at the sun
the baptism of thought
he told her, the thought is blessed,

by the sound the birds, frighten and depart
as winds and words, they scatter us
I live in a country, the language
I do not understand, it will defeat itself

it has outlived its songbirds
the bamboo bird cage also. The emptiness

will ruin us. It will bring the house down.
If you could you see the house,
his door opens—

a bed, a desk
and in the realm of a house, his papers—
folded like a flock of birds,
from room to room. As many birds

in cages and white peacocks on green lawn
until a woman said kill all birds, except birds
with white feathers, in no other explanation
but this was no accidental color.

Of all our assassinations which are natural
for us, he said, it is done with the hand,
by converting fingers into tongues words
unspoken are entered, as the birds ethereal—

flight after silver knife cut
a throat, as many words as the transcriber writes
so many wounds the birds receive. A flock,
as elaborate gold saved by the calligraphers

and chrysographers, transcribers—
and illuminators of manuscripts.

Poet you are born with a mouthful
of birds. The doves against the new moon
it is to bring the birds back,
it is to bring back this man (kiss).

To re-enter your text.
Soft emerald eyes.
Consider this color of the eye as beautiful
and the Spanish celebrate it in song—

As the Villancico:
Ay los mis ojuelos,
Ay hagan los cielos
Tengo confianza
De mis verdes ojos.
Que de mi te acuerdes.

Dante speaks of her eyes as emeralds:
Purgatorio, xxxi. I note she has no necklace,
nothing but bare skin at her throat. I can,
says Lami in his Annotazioni, 'Erano I suoi occhi
d'un turchino verdiccio, simile a quel del mare.'

So we talked about scraps of things in gypsy words
Until the touch of his lips is felt—
even when he has gone.

CAUSE OF ABSENCE

Alive as you are willing to be
The verisimilitude of flesh
Ornate and bare and exposed
Hanging in there as the bones tick on

The clockmaker creates these times
Traumatic, jubilant, mournful
Authentic is the crux, seeps out later
Present drags from dust of here and now

You are not the clockmaker
Levitation was the fulcrum
Ransacking single moment
Collapses with weight of fragility

Some life left of your own
Dropping bucket into empty well
It will occupy you in the elsewhere
While bushes burn on the low shelves

Get used to Fire's sermon
As the earth is turning away

Build a new baby on a scarecrow
The shape of the truth

Lean against the fallen wall
Ringing the leaden doorbell—

Why don't I know you?

Recognition of Small Items

Singing from balconies and slums
Arias of heirs and ivory graces
Save us! Where are you now?
Rosaries flung from upstairs balconies
Came rattling down in a hail of stones

Cast back to dark transfiguration
A tricycle nailed to church door
Here and there, a hundred foil eggs
Scattered during the silence of Sunday
So began this merciless December

As rain broke from iron clouds
No more, is time set by the clock-winder
One slight pressure of thumb and finger
A pulse on wrist disappears
Without gloves to touch your face

Without the weakness of hesitation
Give back time to the poor boy
As the clock ticks, the gavel falls
Now the gurney is pushed ahead

Crosses and re-crosses hallways.

Who steals, who trades, the cash amassing
Heirlooms sealed in a security bag
A moratorium of cold or heaviness
All fragile life— fate wills it this way.

AND THE NIGHT IS A REFUGE

Someone left a dream
near the habit of wilder people
the key left on a flat rock at night
guarded by nothing more
there are voices beneath the stairs
an echo if the door slams
this mirror hung upside down
do not look at the mirror directly
seven years bad luck
the children who became wild ones
heard the sound of drumming and singing
riddles and songs
when the future belonged.

THERE IS ORDER HERE

The apparel magnificent
the crown rich
the jewels precious succession
the ornaments exceeding
as a diamond is a stone
maybe the same value
whether set in lead or bone
in the procession
no man can tell when, or how
last day will fall upon him
frame this heart to lasting impression
print black letter of your face
type outline of everlasting trouble
by the way, citizens are continuing
storing miracles in spare rooms
hallowed grace of hawk and hound
there is a firmament overhead
I see a roof but no walls
everything is about to change
as you taught me on closing cue
the way to heaven is a wooden ladder—
the silver threads unwind in the spool.

AOTEAROA

Aotearoa is the savage place, seeding
A heap of broken images, mixing
Mortuary photos with life
But this went further as
Milton sends an Angel
To whisper our chronicle
Opened–mouthed
At the lip of headland
We passed the photo around
The world twice
Something you said
When I come back to you
Mon Angel never return
To this place.

Whose crayons, red and blue
Bruising each perfect soul
Until the color was evidence
Life has its way with us, against
Your body Lover, we went down
Land falling from our skin
Sand falling from your hair.

Passing the headland,
Aotearoa, your sky made me weep,
Even as obscure, clouded places
A flap of wind, flax painted kite—
even as my breath catching, tearing
you away.

Why did I think of this today
In the netting of our nerves
Sharper and sharper
And the spines or skeleton
Poisonous
As you told me later
When we wound
Each other, a slight
Premonition of ruin
The knot, no bigger than a tear
Or a drop of blood.
It had broken off,
But what breaks off can still be felt
In seeds of the spine—
the land belongs to the past.

LAND OF THE LONG WHITE CLOUD

Two floating islands conceived by a whale
Inhabited by monsters and giants
Fished up by a bone hook by one native man
In his dugout canoe, sunfish in flax net
The caul of long cloud white cast
This land in fog, as the sailors enter
The rudimentary harbor with a makeshift dock
A kind of wild tame-less people embark
From the ark of steamship and junk
Dismal omen of the mourning owl
Hissing of feral cats without reason
Bellowing of bulls beyond their season
Our gold was hidden in the hollow tree
Under the harbor bridge girders
While you stood speechless
Only a forgotten person will pause
Whoever held out her arms
Whoever held the lamb-white clouds
You could hear the commuter traffic
And roaring monsters outside the house
In a lonely room of wood and bones
Fame fell under this perverse banner

A dark mansion with strong gate
Where hung a brass bell to sound
Force the ones inside to listen
Casting down the cloud's white cloak
Repellent bells shaking the foundations
Of earth before the hollow voice
Return and make no fiscal delay
For it is true that here it may
Be the dark riddle or mystic oracle
An image of bridge or blood red river
So we search the corners lost for years
After the inquiries, no news lingers
One resolves to travel the world over
To find what was left to find,
Must we wander from place to place
Until our white hair becomes whiter
The years now closed to the ruined
Journey of the endless roads
One thought carried in our mind
Like a stone—
find a remote region to leave our bones.
So, it is not hard to convince myself
that the place where men perish....could be true.
A place in the bleaching of bones
where those who perish are collected as souvenirs by
every passerby and left in a heap. The lost

bones are markers to show the way, guide a road
through the land for future travelers on the pathway
 (no) moa bird are visible in the air, (no) kiwi or weta,
or stink beetle on the earth; traces of nothing
and in places signs of life departure, piles of sad
bleached bones unidentified—
as man or animal.

Quarter Acre Paradise

They have stolen places I owned,
our palaces,
the lakes of my eyes
the river between us

the art of stealing so many
things belonging to me, stolen

There is a cannon in the garden
surrounded by purple lilac
there is cold blood in our hearts
I did not wish these things

Our palaces towed on a barge
to the edge of pacific ocean
burned on the water all night
ivory gates open for cremation

Now places seem foreign
along the road
in an altered landscape
such places make me weep

Is anything left
in a handwritten note about sadness
litter on a strangers lawn

When the world wears a woman's tears
there are memories speaking
the abacus of wooden beads
each one faint sandalwood
it's a trick of the visionary
an apocalyptic perfume of fate
like the candle end of time—

I did not memorize these things.

VISITOR AT LARGE

The island keeps us awake,
With inclement rumor
All of this was before Pascal's Gambit
You would not know her

The island keeps us awake,
Strangers admitted. No family invited
All of this was before Pascal's gambit
Poverty seasoned by temporary dreams

All sorts welcomed. Before you lost inclination
Only the preparation, the expectation greater
Poverty is seasoned with temporary dreams
Extortion not far off, we broached five years of lies

Only the preparation, the expectation greater
The kindred re-named in the hallow
We stand before the deserted quarry
As if a diamond is a stone of the same value

Over come in distress, over worn in years
Whether set in lead or bone

Until the grudge of heart consumed us,
We break the glass of fragility

And if only a makeshift bed; the woman sleeps
When each night takes the day into account
No one would ever believe her dreams.
We begin to break out of fragility

Our private lives open like a book, we were broken
The offer we made at the closing gate
And one hand shades my eyes
Before the painted sky alive with red

Our private lives open like a book, we were broken
Before the painted sky alive with red
The loss enters us like some other shadow
Blackens the pages until we became invisible

And we left a mighty gathering, led by cold ink
We did not know ourselves, after the foreign demand,
Before the painted sky alive with red
People like those, look the other way
In the vespers of the dead, perhaps you misheard

But the people say it is by blind misfortune
Once the devil enters the house like a thief.

TWO DOGS

As far as the eye could reach—

It is early in the morning
At the gold-rise of sun
And the lovely mackerel clouds
Too thin to cause predictions
Cast shadows in the sky

There is the bay with not much in it
Except weed and briny water
But the little-selves of circus dogs
Bound through hoops of gratitude
Sit anonymous again

When kindred left the careless
The dreaming of old bones
Plague the dogs like fleas
Like strays without a blanket
We sleep outside of the Master's

And the linen in our fists
As if something else will happen

Every tear from every eye
In every realm of grief
Moves us to another place

It was early morning when I dreamed
you was leaving—
I saw a blue painted boat shaped like a relic
It floated on a smooth sea
But I could not see your face
Because the red sun was behind you—

You seemed to be standing in fire.

DROUGHT

Last month a tap left running
and this month, a bathroom flood
all at once, reservoir and damn
sprinkler, bucket, a watering can
and now, only a trickle is left
and that's the beginning of it
black mold grows like coral
the rest of gray water is loose
in the river's marrow, and I know
there's no end until water is gone
and fish will love the fisherman
tomorrow, river crabs in net
muddied long oars, two, four
and a thought, nothing torrential
you've still got a sink more of water
to wash away the clay
so it goes drop by drop
no rain to dissolve dust
or wash this ash rust
and make vibrant green
grass, like newly-cut jade
new sun almost burns the river

river grass clogs anchor
clouds are empty and flat
apparently a heavenly bottle
will hold tears shed over the land
to remember the rivers' tributaries
lake and moratorium, each salted ocean
the morning there is no rain
I think it is strange—
How the nature of water can change.

PAPER-WRITER

The moon, centurial lantern of thought
Rises over houses where fishermen are at prayer
The sea resounds with spirits before dark wave
As night deepens over the moonless island

Everything is as you make it

Ghost dogs warn drowning to come
The sea draws back to the edge of world
Breathless creatures like bait on a hook
Fishing-boat lights flicker green, and are gone

Every fish must hang by his own gills

Moon illuminating disaster's displacement
Shines like an iron mask above brothel and bridge
The moon a troubled witness of ocean's erasure
Sinks into nights entanglement and is gone

Every man is son of his own words

In the ebb and flow of mystery and misery
Reverie of sand and ripple of oar
A shipwreck of a thousand times
In long line of sadness, a thought
The same moon sparkling on the Andaman long ago

Millions of beautiful human eyes have looked out to
sea—
And now they are gone

Everything as you take it.

PLATH'S RIVER

Two women in boat,
crossing the pathways of water
oars drawing into a deeper part,
the calm and the blind
beginning and beyond
as the river divides
as if one can turn
back to beginnings
instead of following the river
and traveling onwards,
as mysterious blue
flows to higher ground
we belong to origins
born amid a stand of churches
Thirty-seven Holy islands
empires of the ancestors
you may think in that deep
clear water an illusion
carried away time unfolding
our hands dipped in blue ink
but it is the color of your eyes
scrubbed clean by tears

your cotton shirt, intensely blue,
weighted with Plath's river stones
that held us under.

DOWN ON HIS LUCK

I hear your voice from the after room
Something old and pernicious
Don't forget, please don't forget
Cruel thoughts to confront
That is the epiphany of mind

A man starts a fire under gum trees
I see the whole landscape burn
Struck by antique tinderbox
How detail came back to life

The oil and linseed and handmade canvas
Out in the bush plainer
Sit down while the water boils
Looking at your clothes from every angle

Suddenly afraid of being forgotten

Overcoat missing military buttons
Seeing you from the perspective of an outsider
You ask if there will be singing in dark times

By the time you pour billy-tea in a tin cup
The choir was singing *about* the dark times
And a hundred years later,
When a stranger looks at the painting—
You are sitting there.

ABOUT THE BURNING

There are rules for making a winter fire
If you have nothing else to do
Make fire-lighters with evening's news
Set pine sticks like a variant tent
But only when the fire is breathing
Do you shovel black coal and maleficence

This before burning fires lost the moon
Left no green in the blackened room
Rude light cast by the circle of sun
Gospers Mountain a puzzled pyre
Also Brooklyn and Ferryman's Ridge
As smoke smothers Gustave's Bridge

Buckets flow over with givers cash
As houses fill with particulate and ash
Enter the refuge for dogs and thieves
Yesterday's bread stolen from corner store
Silhouette of baby sleeping with a paper mask
Even as lightning kept the world awake

But the Raptor bird sends jewels of embers

To flush prey hidden in drought spun grass
Transience and permanence, hot smoking stack
See the Tasmanian wolf rest on long way back
Now a million canaries no longer sing
A billion bees forget to make comb-honey

A match was lit in the Blue Mountains
Tourist tickets tempered smoke
Now Three Sisters vanish in guilty dispatch
Carpe diem in this hellfire hits back
Wild heart inked by the devil in sand
Strong-arm an island as coveted trophy

Red land inferno reached only by air
Drag water from the swimming hole
Put on feather shoes and point the bone
As the white dingo swallows the stones
Our cloud drifts into churches in Chile,
Returns home the cinders and ashes

Fire retardant pink as circus floss
Stains Saint George's cross
Pink melts into Southern stars and Alps
As dogs die of thirst in the marginal squalor
Since the sacred blue changes course
We drink wild water of brackish origin

Speak muddied words before we leave
Enter the refuge for wild dogs and thieves
Put on feather shoes and point the bone
Pay the piper for loss of home
When islands become relics of fear
Sacred red rock reached only by air

The red light cast by the circle of sun
There is no green left on blacked hills
Even as the houses soot and particulate fill
As the cinders smother Gustave's Bridge
The lake upside down filled with dust
This since the burnt desert found us alone

This as the white dingo turns to stone
But what if I see children outside the river
What if wildfires catch clothes and hair
What if there is nothing left to repair
This ending is the beginning of extinction
A billion marsupials in the book of the dead

For all this, a child from the cold land said
Come into the café from the side-street
Open the morning paper and weep.

ESCAMPS

There are pigeons in the woods, the
hum of wasps in the fig tree outside
there was a saint who tamed animals
and wild birds, who opened the door
of the Ark a thousand years away
he was smiling the day
I signed on as pilgrim
and then I traveled with him
I traveled with fire
warm ash left in the fire-place
the only clue that we slept here last night—
the rain has thinned out.
I am not sure if you are
a disciple, a pilgrim, sent like sleep
to erase my own thoughts.
I am note sure if my stone jar of dreams
is adulterated by you?
if you borrow my shadow and walk
farther than I had been
would you find your way back
without a compass
tell me what you had seen?

I will put these prayers in my shoes
and walk a thousand miles
with my eyes closed
but I'll always come back to you.

CLOSE TO THE MUSEUM

I remember when our gate
was unbolted by the man
more suspicious than fires
he held the seeds of ruin
such truth blackens night
blacker than tar or pitch
until he shadowed us
until we became invisible
sentiment ruins and perishes
will you lie to escape jubilance
a hundred palm leaves kept
folded like origami crosses
kingdoms that come will go
in the rebirth of familial misery
there is no word of forgiveness
It cost three thousand pounds

to stop the dog from dying
it cost ten thousand pounds
to build a dry course wall
to dampen traffic sound
it cost five hundred pounds
to start the pendulum swaying
and in the heaving of rocks
forty cruise ships weigh anchor.

But now his garden where day and night
bring no human sound
apples grow through their blossom
and the garden statue is sent blind.

WHERE ENDS MEET

The act of disappearing is easy to do
so many goodbye's and good night's
but it was the last word we said
with the roses in Fire and Red
left our memories to each other

there was no need to guess
where to look for our bones
the marrow of the truth
it was better to die with you
than to live the year without

then there is the question
what to do with our bones
if water is the beginning
the debt of our bodies
submits to endless streams

A piece of boat burned Pompey
our bones the smoke to follow
wandering blackened landscapes
when it comes to dark midnight

crack open clouds and beg the crow
to end this Fire with ashes

Now the pyre a hundred feet high
and if the wind should change direction
it is art puts life back in our bones
if water quenches the Soul
let none fear their drowning.

FOR SHADOWS

There were too many bodies
Blackened with tar or pitch
Remains of commonplace people
Dressed up in cheap resinous attire

They loaded mothers' one by one
On steamboats in the midday sun
First one, then another didn't matter
In the end all dead were rotten

They burned in no particular order
Mummies for fuel instead of coal

What time has past avarice consumes
Wife, sister, mother, daughter
Are you asleep or are you dead tonight

Still the King lays untouched
Wrapped up in sweet confection
Myrrh, frankincense, ambergris's
Away from the smoke in the wind
Under sand and pyramid

Like the boats along the River Nile
All things impermanent pass away
The medicine treats the wounds
And the Pharaoh is sold for balm

Someone waits on the other side
For the Soul's promised return.

GONE TO BUSH

All grass was burning when I looked back
The author of human graves was watching me.
I caught his eye like fire on the edge of the earth...

A dry October, a dry November,
there was rain between
the sound of a match strike
you made the burning bush

you were the mortuary host
take this shipwreck of fire
what everyone says must be true
you cannot convert an arsonist

revenge is a kind of wild justice
a flaming arrow fired towards
a fixed point, is nothing
but an impulse received from the archer

the point reaches its end
as though of its own making
codes of fire, laws of fire
all alight set by delusion,

whosoever studies revenge,
keeps his own wounds green
time came and took fire dancers
back to the burning lands,

shooting flames wild orange flay
hideous wind moves to trouble it
dancing in heavy boots,
dancing in heavy boots—
we only salvage what remains.

FOR THE RECORD

In the home of dark objects
The loss is never cured
Everything takes on smoky hue
This habit of leaving windows open
When severe deeds are done

Bone and skin, you were the reason
All flesh and blood has cruel season
Outside the crows ascend from houses
The black crows against phantom light
Dropping feathers in delinquent spiral

Shaped the misery of the dwellers within

The air is still, until ominous blackbirds
Rise up in one telltale column
Smoke rises from our own roof
Why wicked bless the pretender
Fireplace with displaced ember

Fanning a thousand reasons
Until every family remembers

Moment of constant ash
An epigram of greater wasteland
But this was justified by summer

And all of a sudden merciful

Crimson are the Christ trees
Their purple branches, however old
Spreading themselves along the cliff
Adornment for the ruined

Old wreaths for our ghosts.

THE MESSENGER

When day and night passed unnoticed
I saw the devil by the ancient door
Through the curtains of quartz rosary
He spoke where no blood can reach

So far as the living may be
He remarked that excess happiness
Was something to extinguish

Now the fires burning out of his domination

And day-by-day dead leaves fall and melt
We held mirrors up to the blackening skies
While glooming ashes razed the screams
A billion mammals smolder in deep thicket

Lilies and white gladioli close our throats
Dancers and coiners of dreadful things
We are the voices of our past requiem
Which must be the lives to be

If two shadows chance to met face to face
And ask and ask with lips of the dying
And who are you?
I do not know if the body's rage and poison
Is compensated by fire in the soul

For the hollow ghost blames the living
In the last word there's a secret kept
That will never let me rest
I only know I died last night
In the elysium field
As the truth is spoken—
there is no living with or without you.

WAYS THROUGH

Lifting its snows into foreign sky
I have seen Friday's moon
Rise like a disc over hill
Illuminating the circle of gold
Halo on pale marble
Still face of a sleeping child
Before the blood-red morning
And snowy mountains white against
The red sky, where there are birds
That rested on the day after
There are moments of self-importance
A red blanket folded like wings
For all I know—
The same woman that lures you here
Causes you to trip lures you away
And in the open fan, with its audacious sun
Day of blood that is about to be
That is all perplexedly
So whoever sees will never forget—
all things red, burn in memory.

WIND OF THE EAST

Under black flag
where black crows fly
war stallion takes rider
in fierce race until
silver chains on his wrists
resound like clashing blades

He has caught sight of her
her silk glimmering silver
under the war mask, he smiles
such luck in presence of jade
behind him still dark of night
before crimson morning fades

Sharp cut relief against dark armor
and you must understand
that this is intended as a picture
you can tell either by birth or blood
only through armor and objects of art
or Durer's hands carved for prayer—

You were the man who knew

the woman of the past
warmed her body near your heart
as you opened your arms
to set her free, whispered:

All must remove their masque
Take care who you pretend to be.

GARDEN OF OPIUM

I wet bamboo with rain and made a flute—
whoever hears it falls in love
tell me you hear a faint song
when I play late at night
or have I traveled too far away

I burned sea-grass to ash
mixed with salt, it makes water taste like sea—
whoever drinks it falls in love
I saved a cup for you.

I touched the gull that swallowed arsenic
I rubbed my hands over its wing

now everything I touch becomes invisible
time touches us—but we can't see it.

I cut a deep incision in the bark
I carve into the trunk of a mango tree
the owner of boat and oars
no name, can I write but yours.

You kissed me all those years ago
what was it you wanted from me back then?
your body under baroque quilt,
trail of tendrils and frayed oak leaves

Original feelings of our beginnings
beneath crewel branches
embroidered birds of paradise
Chinese figures stand guard outside
lemon-wood pagodas.

There are golden threads at lands end
in remembrance of the years before
on the island of small elephants—
the ones who remember...
the ones who forget.

DUMAS

The dying day, the retreated sun
red death of the day-star, sun death
all the waters of the Eastern Rivers
dyed with the blood-red sinking sun

The moon as a funeral lantern
first to carry sun's funeral in this way
and the procession of stars that follow
are the long-path of mourners' tea-lights

Do you remember the antique places
Old Bridge of prostitutes and thieves
now ghosts assemble in shadows there
paper lanterns sojourn dark waters

Then a lovers' moon rises for starlight
and the heart geometrizes everywhere
through the finely woven bamboo screen
he divines his fingers touching her there

And as the fan opens with its red sunrise
all reflections turn water into plum wine

far from flooded rice fields on a day of blood
all that is packed in sugar and salt will not rot

On a ribbon of blue silk there rises a red sun
that same gold-spattered day-star
burns into memory like opium
whoever sees it will never forget

Her dark eyelashes open like a fan.

THE FORGIVEN

The sacred blue let down into the lake
islands springing from the lotus prayers
the mother dreaming where the cradle stood
the water bearers holding hands

and here the echo of prayer over the land
blue cathedrals hold relics of the heart
to be reached only by footpath
the bailiff adds up our days of absence

less miracles of the Ark of Covenant
silence starts the Ten Commandments
the travelers who converse with Our Lady
or Mary of Zion in seventy-fifth dialect

Here, under the Bodhi Tree, a newborn baby
asleep in a wicker basket, if only by her cry, the
Temple Monks' shall find.

ANDAMAN ISLAND

Volcanic rock barters with waves
And while I stood on shale beach
I saw the demon stalking about,
Selling drugs to ward off an earthquake
A handful could be bought

It happened that the tsunami
Came the day after Christmas
The earth listening to the wave
The widows with no other way
Of letting go sorrow, planted frangipani

In the end, they value the tree more
For being full of perfume,
More than white blossoms
Covering the graves like wedding clothes

Now sadness haunts our island
It is not a fault of the season
The nutmeg blossoms are full
Yellow and ruddy in rusted splendor

Everything that has been long dead
Conveys itself to us in the breeze
You do not leave— someone lets
You go: she whispered.

Do Trung Lai's Shirt

Confucius Temple has two roofs

A chinoiserie of flying eaves and tiles
Solidly fired in sanguine clay
Dragons decorate the beams with fortune
But the bodies are placed
So that the entire beast cannot be seen

When the temple was searched,
Poems were found for us
In the shadows of real things
As the fortuneteller floats lanterns
On the dark water

Our dreams burning longer than desire

We collect documentation of dreams
I hold *Five Lakes in Bac Minh Province*
The lake that is most erotic
Your poem, Do Trung Lai
Translations of the old wind

But in the image born of my breath
Like the Tam legend from Eau River
Wash a Poet's heart and out it comes
I read your river poem from the center
At the heart of the circle

For one's actions in life may be compared
To tossing stones in a pond
Looking into the Well of Clarity
In the Temple Garden,
Seeing through a seam of ancient jade

No sooner has a pebble fallen into water
It transforms into a small circle
Which becomes a larger circle
No one lives in isolation
The circle continues to expand
Until it covers the entire pond

There are ghosts throwing stones

Ghosts listening
When someone is reading
And their voice becomes drowsy
Turning vegetables into mint
The silent burial of words as soon as I speak

Bamboo boats turn into dragon boats
River turns into dragon wine of a thousand years

If translators are architects of image,
Do I use the force of vocabulary,
Not simplify,
One lake to sink love-sickness.
 Do I soften edges to a kiss
As I read *a lake of water red, like lipstick*

Shall I bar translation of valuable texts
Tear them up so that you can clean your feet
An ink stone with such a hard surface,
That the stick glides over it,
Without leaving any deposit of ink
You write *That river has only one color*

Who can read your poem without in some way
Becoming the river?
What does translation prove?

Your words are merely lent to me
No wall, no rope, no string can hold your words here

Tomorrow when all Poets disappear—
We that have read poems
In the belief that we could understand each other
But flesh and bone are rivers
That separates us into distinct and lonely regions

If one lifts the door a little while leaving
There is no sound
It is sad to think that our words
Indifferent to our leaving,
Should remain unspoken after we have gone

Shall we cast off disguises that produce no poem
And return to the coats we put away,
And a lake to wash the four-part traditional shirt,
To wash the headband,
To wash the back silk pants

And as I thin the pages left behind,
I catch the faint scent of lotus,
Which seems quite occidental
Do Trung Lai's shirt all faded blue
From sunshine and the dew

Intoxicated in a garden nameless and eternal
The way he goes away in search of two sides
Of a leaf or a blade of grass—
please wash them in one separate lake.

JADE

Sap of the lac tree rises
In the mandrake of village
Rain drums beat out a long life
Under the saddle-shaped roofs

Finials on resistance pole
Polished like silver-rayed star
Bell and chime stone
Announce our coming, like a comet

But rice is thrown on hot stones
Until black deflects the sun
As crane birds appear in mist
We hid our wealth in rice fields

Like a jade suit for mourning

For a small body of believers
Having neither homes nor cities
You cannot strip a naked man

Like aristocratic hostages
Hide under a moth-worn blanket
This nakedness will pass
Pieces of old not to be classified
As treasure for antiquity
But appropriated by the authorities—
mere bodies without substance.

In Red

Focus on antlers and tusks
Mandibles and teeth
Dangerous parts of us
Solitary hunters of obsidian
Migration was black ribbon
Until blood dropped red
When beast was carved up
No man knows the animal in us
The terrifying motif
Such scavenging desires
Baiting a stone bull
Hunting a red deer
Evokes a man with a red ink stone
How he captures animals in his mind
A painting for the rock to keep.
Enough to shelter the animals also
Outstretched wings hover
Wild words and wildness
Skull, blood, bones
Like thunder clouds—
shaking Sappho's stones.

THE DAYDREAMER

In a hammock under cashew bough
The siliceous painted patterns
Shade her eyes with other light
Above her the moving frames

Bullets of black parrots
Rare as solitary thought
Passing over this secret place
During the season of mosaic

Each world of delicate engineering
A first time for every moment
The trees may be old
The blossoms are always new

The nut skin grow poisonous
Why the medicine tastes of bitter
Millions of winds released
The great flock of birds

Fly up in a dust parabola
Rising like an ominous blanket.

THE NATURE OF FIRE LANDS

Blue gums grew, blue gums fall
Fire weaves the black ravens
Who haunt the threads of existence
Fortunes kept in the indigenous stars

One thing follows another after the retelling
This genesis fits firmly like a mask
Before the mirror of history
The voice of birds unfolded in the flame tree

Satan and Faust mouthed this deed
Cover the mirrors silvering patinas
One hand shielding my eyes
As the earth betrays its owners trust

The night we sleep on a pillow of sand
Embers from the Raptor bird
Out of this world where ash is ablaze
Flutter from incendiary trees hoary night

And Icarus returns with his sealing wax
Fly all birds into the atmosphere,

No bird can reach the eye of heaven
To look at the world, full of contradictions

A red sky, its back against the moon
A billion small creatures dead from the flames
Thinking of what is, at different times
Not knowing the clockmaker has gone
Who is master of the future?

The sound of a hundred dogs barking
Black mosaics in the New Year shadow
We pointed to the blue arcade of bay
A dozen or more whales
Like a mighty gray congregation—
An omen that rain was on its way.

IRON FLOWERS

Quiet memory is a private place
I know the faraway corners of you
We were never to be weighted down
I have looked the other way
I have swallowed the stone
Everyone that has been long gone
Hypocrisy was a cruel device
Strikes a hell of denial
Your cold judgment unfortunate
Discriminates nothing except
This thirst for reclamation
Among the damn of profanity
Amidst the curse of human hope
Rain outside the door
Traffic on the road
A man still hostage to misfortune
Until he forgets the connection to patterns
&routines & layout of city
Everything becomes a painted garden
It's the second life that grows the soul—
And this is why we thank you.

THE MAPMAKER

What to do at the end of life to unweave
The tangle of our existence
What left to be decomposed by worm
To leave last parcel of our composition
As if the burdens were sufficient for a garden
We may carry our own compost

The dead are all alive in the world
Yet less than ghosts they speak a little
Of things past and things to come
But not one word for the present
Except for the blood that makes a living
And fear of broken and mangled things

The living too afraid of ice and poppy
Asks what will happen to his only son
Thin habit with a thought like a blade
Far beyond the force of weaponry
So small they end, so they begin again

Forgiven dead put away their malice
And meet with perfect shadows

Never the ghost of a killing spree
Or broken into the factory
Who trained the dogs of fate

Light makes the visible seem invisible
Except for homeless in the crucible Mall
Aimlessly wandering hallowed Hall—

What is it like to sleep on the ground
Like a dog without a blanket?

FIGHTING THE LAUGHTER

In hallucinatory streets
Sydney homeless are fatigued
Even the labeled are invisible
Blood with no outlines at all
Haunted in the theatre of lack
The spirit addicted to dreams
Peaches, figs, expensive truffle
Track the trauma of lost
Between mother and child
Body, blood, emblazons soul
Illustrating a needle's point
In the name on a forearm
Or star, rain, bird, sun, fish, tree
Each quiet secret be trapped
And when you speak of time
Cold outlines, clear labels
The shock has lingered
The protest goes on
Terrible the naked candle burning
On our mothers' graves
Such bad makes us remember
And never-never understand

In the unconscious, we were all similar

All aware of darker regions

Dirty bats came from the red caves

One never will know

Till black thought will wash

Over memories we tow

And all the dark centers

Of the memory of loss, endless

Should render one incapable

Everything from the neck up

Devoted to this revolution

Take for mine

Everything from the neck down

Lover and lover and lover

Of love or any other human feeling—

except this fear and the need for one another.

MELBOURNE WINTER

The monster in this native slum
Is the leader of the gang
Abandons all that reminds him
Of past in which he is fixed

It is to this hell always in his
Bad thoughts weave together
With fragments of remembered liturgy
That his soul descends to steal a breath

Last seen on a Saturday night
Outside the comedy club
Darkness under his overcoat
With a magnum ordered online

During the plausible interval
The women with valuable faces
Double and multiply
Even the labeled are the same

With no outlines at all
How can you tell one from another

Telescoped wit, funny and amusing
Distortions, puns, double-talk confusing

To the mobile phone and belly-bone
Woman, a child or two in the womb
Until the unconscious shows itself
Come the floods of unnatural fantasy

Apples, flames, doors, houses, tent
The theatre of laughter silent content
The consummation of violence
Revenge red pistils of tragic roses
In buds of steel bullets
Split, vanish, solidifies the embodied—
close the mouth of every witness.

THE ANARCHIST

Flint axes, bronze swords, a red dress
The historian's embarrassment increases
The abundance of documents at his disposal
Through the evidence of a simple life

It is admitted without much hesitation
When events were recalled by two witnesses
But all evidence is contrary and irreconcilable
Preferring one piece of evidence to another

The crowd passes over the cobblestones
Although some are slower, the delay of old
The mother with a child while all the while
Carol singers high on soprano

And the same old sleigh-bells tied with string
For everyone knows golden stars, silver angels
And mistletoe at the city of crossroads begins
Ten thousand useless things

Every day the astronomical clock chimes
Twelve carved apostles, the eyes and ears of God

Go marching around in front of the Christ
The protest goes on while the devil smiles

As the man in the dark coat walks the landmass
Between four canals, past towers of the ramparts
Where great armies marched
In walked one man and then another

As all hearts will change forever
Six men lost and six men wanted
For the creation of new ghosts
As the last water of our fountain turns into blood
Unnoticed the moon fell out of the sky—
we lost time instead of gaining it.

THE TELESCOPE

Everything has its own shadow—
Like an old woman learning an alphabet
I wrote a long letter for you
I had no time to make it shorter
The months fading like bride's tuberose

For our lives, it is said; the universe spawned
From a limitless abyss with nothing in it
An area of confusion between dark
This was chaos, the progenitor of all things
Pandemonium—so we crawled out of it

I wished as you wished
Poured out words to the wind
You may wish, but never possess
We came with the cornucopia of Gods
Embraced the approaching luck

Confronted a mass of Saints, more Angels,
Some owed us more than nothing
Some own us more than we know
Some searched for us since we were younger

Compasses a million years out of date—
still they find us.

It happened to be like a bird in a cage
Left outside we despaired of getting in
And those on the inside desirous to get out
We held dreams, so they were taken—
But chaos of the past gives no directions
Thousands of names never reached high ground—
and the speechless graves followed.

In August

Who will forget day unlucky
When unmasked pilgrims
With coercive impulse
Sat astride the leaden horse
As death's breath drifted across
The historic enslaver
In this unfortunate calendar
The years of coercive error
Now the harvest went to seed
Tainted rice poured down the gutter
The white of a million shrouds
Barbiturate in bathwater
Heroin in the tub
Cocaine down the drain
Better not to be born
Now days are complicated
And the earth is an empty husk
With little left inside of it.

BLACK DOG

From memory we begin again
all moments are taken
like an image in a photograph
in the photograph lies a dead dog
I have no way of stopping this thought
a small harp set at the entrance
of its breathing, a sixth sense,
the movement was delicate,
it starts as a whimper and moves
beyond all limits, the ghost dog
another month is ending,
the barks of one hundred dogs
but none can match a single whimper
amber preserves a butterfly,
the way we preserve memory,
imagine nothing is extinct.
It is only us forgetting what was.

THE DISTANCE

There are rules about being associated
but you do not know what they are
I walked around with your voice in my head
if there were rules remember
they are only there to be broken
you must prepared to use the flags
of metaphor like a semaphore
you must be prepared for the awkwardness
of holding opposing thoughts
if you have thought this through
the great ones break the rules on purpose

To break

To buy

To crowd

To drag

To horde

To lock

To queue

To stare

To swipe

To touch

To wipe

to steal food from blind woman's cart
in machine-gun leap of consciousness
to be stuck in fever of *You, You, You*
to fondle peaches not yet ripened
I reset difficult, terror, tough, violent
last serenades on twisted balconies
strikeout lies after your voice has gone
ask poor families to light incense
for a stranger's photograph on the alter
next to every mother and daughter
offerings of rice and tea will continue
but so what of son's sentimental eulogy
when the virus offers no apology
we who witness needle and vial
strike out lies after voices are gone
you who got away with everything
step into that elsewhere—
and explain yourself.

MIDNIGHT MOJAVE

Now that your road is mine
its unlimited length of dust
the blinding plains of night
to keep your eyes from my face

old stones, blue fires of fate
the exact moment hypnotized
I have absorbed the thirsty core
and what is more

I have already described
the muscle and bone of raw
feeling, the reason I dress in a hurry
and cannot leave this Lover

love of the road the blinding arias
stitched with sand and dust
saying yes
and the filigree of night

held the ancient coin
the blackened one they toss back
and it lands on the road
the face looking up

I find myself falling
deep into your beautiful words
blurring my senses to everything
your voice magnetic

a strong pull opens up—
and all that is inside
I see the dream
between the worlds

saying yes
the remains of life we keep
all we have left belongs to us—
inside another sleep—
night runs again.

THE PREMONITION

Father is ninety-two years—
The choir birds of dawn's
Chorus the vivid passing
As needle remembers the vein
Winter holds his face
The icy fingers next to the
Bosom of air. Too much
Sound
The rattle of bone china
Cups blossoming roses and imperfect
Cracks in wedding china
Biscuits and money hidden in jars
Too much remembering
My heart does not break but
One day it will.
A closet of secrets
Papa—I look and wait
For it with a thin purse
A folded photograph I almost
Burned with your phone number
The pyre you made of wedding clothes
Belonging to mother

Sepia atonement the
Bruised rawhide- clasps
Rusted on the enclosure
Found in a thicket after
The burning. Knocking on
Your door, waiting at your bedside.
What unsatisfied longing for the
Irish nurse whom your
Eyes follow around the room
Already you are in love with
Her wild red hair afraid to talk to her
I am not happy
Or unhappy, just waiting as
Usual
Where's your wife in
Your imagination? Too many
Eyes watching your face
Watching you
Sleep and waiting for
You to leave us alone.

Waiting for someone to go
Like listening to grass grow
Like waiting for water to boil
Like watching paint peel
Like hearing the bell toll

Like waiting for bell to bellow
The organ music to fade
A lot will be taken from you
The ties, suits discarded
Small sadness and heartbreak
An open soliloquy
You said, a friend you can trust
Morphine in brusque manner
Makes vision from floral curtains
Beyond living room
Beyond walled garden
Where yellow roses Mother planted
Exist beyond boundaries
Of your home country
You brought distance along
Developing your wings on the way over

Below the grass
Beyond all forgiveness
There is order here
A lot of satin and dirt
If you don't get it right the first time—
go back and begin again.

In Search of Nobody

Nobody helps you

Nobody in front of you

Nobody behind you

Nobody can advise you

Nobody is there

Nobody cares

Nobody sacrifices

Nobody remembers

Nobody delivers

Nobody hopes

Nobody reminds you

Nobody says

Nobody is kind

Nobody is impressed

Nobody waits for you

Nobody loves you

Nobody has

Nobody will

Nobody needs you

Nobody whispers in your ear

Nobody sheds a tear

Nobody helps

Nobody can breach the tunnel
Nobody will teach you
Nobody will save your ass
Nobody will understand
Nobody wins
Nobody saves the world
Nobody can forgive you
Nobody says ecstasies
Nobody opens the magic box
Nobody's blood is yours

At the end of it all
Oh there has been weeping
And walkouts
In the breach of a foil
This most of all
In the most silent part of night
Facing the dark wall
Nobody is stopping you
Nobody gives a damn
Nobody answers
It's just yourself you have
When nobody is there.

ON MONDAY

Death needs a beautiful face
it is addicted to its own
rampant hunger
shatters the pulse
breaks the breath
in the bloody tangle
stole her sad heart
the hands that hold
now suddenly cold
as dust gathers itself
death's conquering complete
her smile stiff as an uncut ribbon
without a word of leaving
opiates trace a glass
life dissolves on death's
ancient tongue—

If suicide note is not a riddle or a clue— two old
women, tell us please, the answer.

INTERLUDE

Fly all you black parrots
Flutter like flags on the trees.

Tell me about the photographs—
As the weeks ran out of miracles
The rain set in with severity
First, it rained, and then it snowed

Although a gilded year was promised
It seems an impossible intent
Then it froze, then it thawed
Then it rained again

Take your black umbrella home
The salutation if you, if you will go
For in such Satan-like months
That's how our lives are spent

A reason to leave, a place to stop
The journey in-between
We stand between hemispheres
Of Arcadia and the butterfly effect

The rule of passing is clear
Keep to the left, and you're sure to be right
But if you keep to the right, you'd be wrong
The sand is sunk, the glass is out

The sun from the sky gone
We go to bed and wake in another world
With the children at our feet
First a boy, then a girl
Circles are small and yet complete

All you were, and all you are to me—
the man with his name written on water.

LOVE IN A TIME OF COVID

Each night next to my own body
In a garden full of opium
Some confirmation of us,
When something feels so lost
Back from the vanishing point
In the process of disappearing
Your arm across my chest
Heavy like a folded wing
That is what fate means:
to be facing each other
and nothing but each other
and to be doing it forever
& words reveal nothing
& silence is not recorded
While they chronicle a million deaths
Before the sextant takes the spade
Now the whole world is a graveyard
In a death-garden of unmarked tombs
Abacus of stones, infinity of earth—

all I ask is a little pause in this suffering.

SOUTH WEST ROCKS

A room empty of heat this winter
Unadorned for the dreamer's taste
A seat made of old stone

"Many a day sat with one another
And hand in hand like the immortal
Until the seas go dry
And the rocks melt with the sun
I will love you still
While the sands of life shall run."

Walking back to his room
Like Jesus and the desert fathers
She was barefoot on the stones
A photograph developed slowly
Soft blue light
In the photograph
A loaf of bread and carafe of wine—
living with you—more beautiful than ever.

INKER OF VEINS

Counting the years lost
Like rings on a mango tree
I saw a blue tinge like a halo around every thing.
These, love letters, more passion, than microfilm
Could hold—adulterate my thought, hides
More secrets, contains more acts than
Your body could verify, where, your hands
Touch, pale skin and silk broke,
Where musk, from the broken vial,
Breathe the perfume on a throat.

—I am a room in a disused brothel
A red candle stolen from a church,
The edges of the atrium,
A wound, where
All love ends and begins again.
A stone jar of dreams, tiny scar on a heart,
The face of a man, foreign postcard,
Souvenir maps wrapped old feelings
-I am a vault where this blueness stays, the ink,
Line of thread, embroiderer of parchment—
inker of veins.

MATERNAL GHOST

She is lying there in the interval
waiting and even if I pressed the clover
or a flower between the book and
the room, air is measured
in lilac and violets
wind in the velvet,
smells of her perfume
the purple tracery on the green stem
the web in narrow splinters.

She is bone and wool
treasure casket purple cloak
 rag and calcified relic
of a resurrected saint
to hear your voice as solitary choir
to see your face smiling at the window
the halo. Highly glazed. It shines as if
I held a candle to it
Even the sound
When she dropped a coin in the box
Disappeared—
one does not imagine this.

A Note From a Foreigner

The hypnotic apocalypse surprised us
Then when I reread as witness
It was love that contains loss
As a premonition
Trickling between my blood
A remembrance of the past
A microscopic life
A slide of champagne bubble
the hum of a finger
on the rim of a glass
or was it a jar of cicadas
These are an invention,
A weak composition
There is form in all things
Revelation exists as this, tricking
Me into tying secrets to myself.

But I remember around eleven o'clock
The courtyard with a fountain
Will always be a ruin for me.
That break of water

The still and foreign chill
Before anyone had noticed
It was possible to witness
This with the naked eye
At the precise moment
The high inner court as
power gathers itself,
penetrates and pervades
and preserves all it traps
before we can figure it out.

THOSE THINGS UNNAMED

For this was the room that took us in.
The edge of a blade, the broken mirror
Razored and worn where luck intersects
This flat paper

A soluble pile of hundred dollar bills
With the face of Jesus.
So when we look in the mirror
We can be anyone

King or a whore
Or a remote possibility
We can retrace our steps from heaven to hell
Make Dante laugh

And Orpheus to cry
Follow the man to Columbia
Who can pull your fate
Through the eye of a needle

If he is right, then I only need
To swallow his bullet

to be his angel.

It happens to be like memory,

A revision of thought

Rewards you just to accept

Your arm, draped like a cloak, around my neck.

FIRST OPERA OF WORDS

It is a birth of dream,
A child of our own possession
Everything, this sacrifice, not safe
From your snares
And wires, in breach of the truth

But who promises her bread, a crust
Who ink in his hand, quenched truth?
Drown the dream carefully
Leave nothing , forget her
Bequeath her nothing
But one day she will be returned to you
In this month of erasure...she resembles you

She was wrapped in rags.
While the rag world is the rag world
Yet perfumed cloth with oranges-flower scent
But then oily stain of bitterest olives
Then who is left to sweep up dead stones,
That penetrate white to her bone
Hold her close, until the rocks of her spine
Belong to your past.

Let my name be traveler, first rains
And you shall be brought down,
and shall speak out of the ground
A voice as low as dust
Shouting out of the stone
We came to you for a little resurrection
When you needed complete obedience
The terrible repetitious history
We had none to give.
In the crush of law in the chain of time
We had nothing to obey.
I will find something in this stony rubbish,
The folded tent unbinding
(come inside and stay) and I will show you
What is left after the losses—
the remains of life, we keep.

FOREIGN CARGO

For a long time
I cannot imagine,
Broken twig of future
Falling out of itself
Carries away the whole dream, wedding
Flowers settling in the minds
Of survivors
A promise of more before everything
Was taken away, what comes out
Of foreign cargo. It carries dreams forever
And now the fortunetellers whisper
Set in the root of the tree
And we ate slices of mango,
I let your arm fall and stood
In the sap and heat, yellow leaking light,
A sacred wood
And dreams still chained to the timbre our soul.

DRAWING IN RED

I was magi of the night
Burning red candles in all the atrium
So they told you to possess me
All my life
I loved you
So many times
Possessed and dispossessed
Enough to make me weep.
I was witness to your heart as it bled
And the way love's binding held us
The tissue weaves tight
So I cried for you
You who holds my dying within himself
I died with you as you were dying
That death was a simple act like leaving—
the breath behind.

DRAWING IN WHITE

The ghosts are self-possessed
They fall dead at the edge of life
They enter the house and spy on us
And hide like children.
They refuse to speak to us
So I asked the saint to pray
For you if you would listen

I lit candles at the alters
In the rooms of the naked
I was witness of the night
Of missing things
The loss reminds us
- I had misheard you
So many times
But this was the broken
Breath, the bad news
Of the worst time that our
Lives knew, the sad
Thing is they did
Not tell us how to live through
An ending and the

Most distinctive
Thing is that I can not
Kill them for destructive
Behavior or force
Him to speak out of his
Bone cold silence. I kissed my ghost—
it feels like snow.

DRAWING ON WATER

I walk on Piha beach, my
eyes shut
But the sun knows how to pass
My sealed eyes and I
can tell that in my world it's
again the sand that engraves
and in my memory I am
thinking of west coast days
except it is black sand in the
letter unfolded and its ink
has yellowed and I
can see your
face beneath the waves,

and the water wakes,
pulling you down like a
dark shell absent from the
earth.

INVENTORY OF PLACES TO DIE

In the winter, you gather newspapers
and these turn into walls in your hand
I pull the roof over you, grasping the tiles
where the night intercedes with stars
& moon
and also those rooms that the city makes
angels in Moscow in some rooms
there are already pillows and puffed feather
blankets and also in some crevasses
winter sheets.

The city gives us many places
cathedral doorway, park bench
public restroom, railway station
a fountain of ice angels
one more is dying
as the snow's falling

Her wing snapped. Broken.
Thirty below zero made leaving easy
the undetermined touch of a feather
a vague feeling in the dead cold
gathered in your arms. Hold me.
But then, if you go before me—
leave the door open with your shoe.

QUEEN STREET

Of our dreams
He tells me to go
I leave
But then I return holding a mirror

And it is a dream
Beyond mercurial silvering
For outside
There were only patterns
Of moon, simple stars
Some seemed to wait
Although the brightest ones
In those days were nothing but

Shadows still full of light

In the folds of mirror
These were only images
Past painted wall, white ceiling
Someone else to live there

Although when I returned
The man was leaving
He did not see us, in the shattering
Whiter than lamb of slaughter

And another snow
But full of ashes
As you, in the act of killing
Bring the flag inside and burn it

Faces blackened by smoke
Loss opens her robe and succors us
Pass around milk that has the taste of ashes.

POEMS OF THE INTIMATE

If you can transcribe the summer heat
in wet syllables around a mouth
it is like this, how you softened
human words to a whisper

in the prison of your lipstick
red mouth
that's where you left, a sweet taste
like a peony flower of red

to transplant it
where you are
but it is not me you are kissing—
it is someone else.

ORIENTAL

A feeling, of mouth and breath,
I know nothing about
The depth of stones and the heart
Or scars from a kiss

I could sense a splinter of naked color
What signs—it is the closeness
Of your perfume that hems your bare neck

This obsession more than carnal flower
On a throat
When the rice paper door opened
A fall of your beautiful shoulder
Its trees budding with lime.

OFF THE TRACKS

The forests of the West Coast hills
are black and red spirits landscape
zinc black kauri cliffs
closer to sea, the hut

band sawed planks sash windows,
a man and a woman look out
on both sides of the track
rows of tea-trees as far as

the eye could see
but there was none of these
red petals that betray summer
the heat of the land burns

each bush to blackened husk
sun sets fierce blood red clouds
a woman looks off into the hills.
she came and went, like wild fire

grass in her hair
he said, I want to hold you

as if he asking her to dance
out of the apocalypse of blacken

bush, sky on fire, gray smoke
like cooking smoke curling
upwards past the river

but then warm hands of the man
on her hips, heat of his body
passing as human warmth through
her thin cotton dress

she looked into his face
as lips burn a long kiss
dedicating the fire to you—
I feel like we are on the other side

I want to say things to you
never said among the living.
there is not much time
I am filled with so much

serene sadness, that is almost pleasure,
I will not forget your face
the way you welcomed me on the threshold
of the house of the dead.

He moved towards her without another
word and he kissed her last time
no longer feel thirst
no longer feel fear

but one thing she understood
separated from each other, we will be like
human dust, particles
rising from the fires into the blood sky—
this is the metamorphosis that waited.

DIVERS MEMORY

What torments me is my thirst
All has been eaten
All has been drunk
We have no water

Wait until this evening.
I do not understand
Translate loss, word for word.
Far from here,
A tap, drips water,

A river runs over
Rocks, fall on soft green moss.
Wet first of all

In the cool of a silent thirst,
She makes the man understand.
I was dreaming about holding
A handful of snow.

Breaking an icicle from roof
But there is a tap—
And above the tap is a card
The water is dirty

We are dying of thirst,
And they put a tap above a bucket.
I will drink if you to join me
Take a mouthful and spit it out,

The water is tepid and sweetish,
With divers memories
With the smell of a swamp
Tadpole spawn and fetid gutter
This is hell, today, in our times,
Hell must be like this
A tap that drips we cannot drink

Wait for something and nothing happens
And nothing continues to happen—
the time passes drop by drop.

FOR FATE

I think of you, how you left a gilded
cage with an open door
and in a prophetic sign of feathers
imagine you have freedom's wings
a thousand laurel branches for luck
I saw fates secret art
beneath the black line of ink
its mystery is known in fortune's cave
at the grotto where you opened
your hand to a woman
the palm was lined with gold
from the light of orient lanterns.

FRAGMENTS OF THE HUMAN HEART

She is standing on the full moon,
whose silver pigment is oxidized
over time, which poet wrote graffiti in tombs
all flesh is as grass the voice said

Cry. And she asked: What shall I cry?
For the past, it is a corpse
what does it mean
this dead and passing thing

I want it back. I want to recover
what is found by another
saffron, mauve and gentian wakes you
with a shower of turquoise and indigo,

the miracle of all these waters
the river, the lake
all her warm skin, against the grass
it could still be felt

only where you stand, keep standing
but after a while, the sound of

someone cutting the lawn
the hard cracking in the garden of stones

summer day, the angel falls —
faraway from yesterday
the ether of grass, the flower fades
but now the spirit blooms upon it
surely the people are grass
there is still the sound of cicadas at dusk—
already there are mimosa petals—
gathering like ghosts in the gardens.

ELLIS STREET

I am the room in a disused brothel, left behind
On the blue wallpaper tiny reindeer orchids.
Women's voices and the ice means something
the crevice deep, slipping against the womb
Arms strong enough to hold us when diamonds
Split.
Apart.

I am carving a garden of sapphire flowers,
the freesias same fragility .
Delicate. Everything that thinks it might perish.
Ravaged gardens. I am in closer to the musk,
breathing perfume on a throat.

Leaves. Stamen. Amorous.
I am absorbing your shape
and all the vague moisture
Skin. Its silk links me to heat and ice,
adulterated
polished, warm hands of a body,
in its arms, the mechanism is beautiful.

When together I figure this sensual math
count every place we touch
everything before and after this
Every reverie with whispered voices
under night arcade like this one

I know nothing about the edge of love,
sharpened for how long the wild nights
the diminishing number of times
this dancing descent or the legend,
slowly dissolving in the white ground.
of you, or anyone, but if they ask me,

I will tell them, what I figured out
the mechanism is beautiful.

Farmers of Sorrow

The farmers of sorrow
They did not like flowers
They burned the trees
And changed the climate—

no one noticed
the chaos in a room
the closure of her mouth
and the opening again
as if testing the ripeness of
of something
just nibbling at pomegranate
fruit, the buds, the dream
we assumed was treasure- fill
in bloom of dusk
we talked for an hour
restored to us, sweet juice
taken in silver chalice
liquid perfumes a mind
sends images to dream
and it seems, nothing wakes her.
Seen as last ridge of city

before river
from which you can never
interrupt this flow
rain clouds after sky
until a sudden downpour threatens
to drown her
like a river drawing all thought
sewage floats into her
the same year
long tears sets this dateline
where the soul must have been.

The farmers of sorrow
They did not like flowers
They burned the trees
And changed the climate—

defying the rules of birth's reward
small gain this falling rain on her.
weaving the water into a palace
river as room
she is gone as a stone
thrown in a river.

THE SLEEPER

In a foreign landscape,
we are ghosts
entering the nights séance
capture what is still unaccounted
immigration beads, the flags of paper
still swathed in wax seal and twine
they speak to us through documents and deeds
in the dust there are everlasting notes
you smell them on the old streets.

One explosion after another
to draw you out of existence
some you hide, others you hate you
use you until they change us
like gunpowder the black, exists
so you can taste it, just a bowl of burned rice
or was it the cave offering a place in the stones
to sleep on the rough earth
pulling the ground around you—

What does it mean to sleep
like a dog without a blanket.

Biography of Susan Blanshard

Poet Susan Blanshard was born in Hampshire, England. She is a poet, essayist, best-selling author, revisionist poetry editor and literary critic. Her nomadic childhood and multicultural past color her writing. Susan has published selected poems such as *'Fragments of the Human Heart'*, and full-length books in poetic prose include *'Sheetstone'*, Spuyten Duyvil, New York and *'Honey in my Blood'*, *'Sleeping With The Artist'*, Page Addie Press, United Kingdom. Her selected poetry and essays are published in numerous international literary magazines including 'The World's Literary Magazine Projected Letters', 'Six Bricks Press', 'Arabesque Magazine', 'Lotus International Women's Magazine', 'ICORN International Cities of Refuge'. 'PEN International Women Writers' Magazine. PEN International Writers Committee The Fourth Anthology, Our Voice', 'Coldnoon

International Journal of Travel and Literature'.

Susan Blanshard is the Revisionary English Poet and Editor for six #1best-selling bilingual poetry books in translation, including the book winner of the 10th Cikada Prize, Sweden. She is the English Poetry Translations Editor for a further sixteen translated works of poetry, literary critiques and short stories. Susan Blanshard is a member of PEN International Women's Writers and Asia Pacific Writers' and Translators'.